Facts About the Griffon Vulture

By Lisa Strattin

© 2016 Lisa Strattin

Revised 2022 © Lisa Strattin

# FREE BOOK

## FREE FOR ALL SUBSCRIBERS

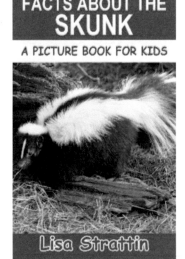

LisaStrattin.com/Subscribe-Here

# BOX SET

- **FACTS ABOUT THE POISON DART FROGS**
- **FACTS ABOUT THE THREE TOED SLOTH**
- **FACTS ABOUT THE RED PANDA**
- **FACTS ABOUT THE SEAHORSE**
- **FACTS ABOUT THE PLATYPUS**
- **FACTS ABOUT THE REINDEER**
- **FACTS ABOUT THE PANTHER**
- **FACTS ABOUT THE SIBERIAN HUSKY**

# LisaStrattin.com/BookBundle

# Facts for Kids Picture Books by Lisa Strattin

Sign Up for New Release Emails Here

LisaStrattin.com/subscribe-here

**★★COVER IMAGE★★**

https://www.flickr.com/photos/kkoshy/28618158311/

**★★ADDITIONAL IMAGES★★**

https://www.flickr.com/photos/gilgit2/49736272548/

https://www.flickr.com/photos/15016964@N02/8486103647/

https://www.flickr.com/photos/tasshu113/4956298683/

https://www.flickr.com/photos/8259447@N06/21016652556/

https://www.flickr.com/photos/steve_childs/48255263496/

https://www.flickr.com/photos/steve_childs/48255273451/

https://www.flickr.com/photos/steve_childs/48255333327/

https://www.flickr.com/photos/seattlecamera/52002730391/

https://www.flickr.com/photos/lennartt/8459608526/

https://www.flickr.com/photos/maccattack2/6178382376/

Contents

# INTRODUCTION

The Griffon Vulture, also known as the *Eurasian Vulture*, is one vulture you can easily identify by its appearance. They are highly social beings, and they like to do all their activities in flocks. Eating, roosting and even nesting are done as a group.

The vulture, as we know, is one of the most famous scavengers, it feeds on carcasses left by other animals.

# CHARACTERISTICS

As already mentioned. the basic characteristic of the Griffon Vulture is that it is a scavenger. The vultures feed on carcasses of dead animals left out in the open, as a group.

Usually, you find vultures making their homes in and around cliffs. The cliffs they like are the ones located away from human population.

They are generally quiet birds; and do not become aggressive without a reason. When they are building their nests or going after food, they can become very aggressive. Even though they eat as a group, they still might fight over the food!

## APPEARANCE AND SIZE

The Griffon Vulture is a large bird. It can measure from 3 to 4 feet in height. The wingspan can be from 7 ½ to 9 feet!

The males of the griffon vulture species weigh around 13 to 23 pounds. The average female weighs 14 to 25 pounds. So, the females are heavier than the males.

The newly hatched babies look just like a smaller version of their parents. They have the stark white small head and small feathers on the tail. The wings are large even on the babies!

# LIFE SPAN AND LIFE STAGES

A very interesting thing about the Griffon Vultures is that they mate for life. This "marriage" can be very long because they live for 40 to 50 years!

During the dating period, called courtship, they like to fly in circles around their home cliffs. So, these pairs, after circling the cliffs, or perching in them, gather a lot of other Griffon Vultures and make up a flock of as many as 1,000 vultures.

The nests of these birds are made of leaves, sticks, and grass. There is a stealth culture among these Griffon Vultures, the females steal items for the nest. They take sticks and leaves out of other vultures' nests and then give it to the male griffon vultures to arrange into their own nest.

The Griffon Vulture does not lay eggs like other birds, it only lays one egg each year. The female sits on her egg for about 3 months before it is hatched.

It takes the baby vulture approximately a year to grow up as an independent bird.

## HABITAT

The Griffon Vulture prefers open areas, like grasslands, where it locates cliffs to build its home. Dry, arid areas are a bonus for them, since those places have an abundance of carcasses that are easy to spot, as they fly around circling near their home.

These vultures have been known to be in Italy, Croatia, the United Kingdom. Israel, Greece, and Belgium.

They used to be found in Germany, but they no longer thrive there. This mass extinction happened in the middle of the 18th century. Although, they were reintroduced to Germany later, they have been found to be declining at an alarming rate.

## DIET

The Griffon Vulture eats any meat it finds, and it only eats meat. They like a fresh carcass as opposed to one that had begun to decay. They dive into a meat carcass as a flock.

Their beaks help them to go deep inside the ribcages where other animals with big open mouths are unable to go. The vultures are cultured when it comes to hunting, they don't attack any healthy animal, although at times they might attack an animal that has been wounded or is bleeding heavily.

## SUITABILITY AS PETS

The Griffon Vulture is a wild animal, and it is also a bird-of-prey. It has a very sharp beak, and its instincts are to kill an already injured animal.

Vultures are not a good choice for a pet!

# COLOR ME

# COLOR ME

# COLOR ME

# COLOR ME

# COLOR ME

# COLOR ME

# COLOR ME

# COLOR ME

# COLOR ME

# COLOR ME

Please leave me a review here:

LisaStrattin.com/Review-Vol-63

For more Kindle Downloads Visit Lisa Strattin
Author Page on Amazon Author Central

amazon.com/author/lisastrattin

To see upcoming titles, visit my website at
LisaStrattin.com– most books available on
Kindle!

LisaStrattin.com

# FREE BOOK

**FOR ALL SUBSCRIBERS – SIGN UP NOW**

**LisaStrattin.com/Subscribe-Here**

**LisaStrattin.com/Facebook**

**LisaStrattin.com/Youtube**

Made in the USA
Columbia, SC
15 July 2024